# THE
# GREEN CARD
# CHESS GAME

*How To Win At Love And Marriage*

## MICHELY SOARES LOPES

PALMETTO
PUBLISHING
Charleston, SC
www.PalmettoPublishing.com

The author and publisher have taken reasonable precautions in the preparation of this book and believe that the facts presented in this book are accurate as of the date it was written. However, neither the author nor the publisher assumes any responsibility for any errors or omissions. The author and publisher specifically disclaim any liability resulting from the use or application of the information contained in this book, and the information is not intended to serve as legal advice related to individual situations.

This book is licensed for your personal enjoyment only. If you would like to share this book with another person, please purchase an additional copy for each recipient. If you are reading this book and did not purchase it, or it was not purchased for your use only, please visit your favourite e-retailer and purchase your own copy. Thank you for respecting the hard work of this author and publisher.

For bulk orders and purchases, you may qualify for discount rates if you email the publisher. Requests for permission to make copies of any part of this book should be submitted to the publisher at contact@michelylopespublishing.com

# TABLE OF CONTENTS

# INTRODUCTION

*"I like to see a man proud of his
country, and I like to see him so live
that his country is proud of him."*
— *Abraham Lincoln*

## THE BATTLEFIELD

In 1940, it became a requirement for foreign nationals to register in the United States. The federal government created a green colored document for immigrants, allowing them to work and live like residents of the United States. Since then, the Green Card has been the dream of many immigrants who want to live legally in the United States.

There are many ways to obtain a Green Card. There's the visa lottery program that welcomes around fifty thousand immigrants from countries where the immigration to the United States is low. Another way is to apply for a specific job, be a refugee/asylum-seeker, or have legal resident family members living in the United States.

The Green Card Chess Game is a strategy I created to make your marriage successful at the same time that you become successful in acquiring your green card. This strategy is necessary because many marriages between American citizens and foreigners are not successful. Relationships tend to result to conflict when not strategized, especially when one partner lacks what the other can provide. Playing the green card chess game will turn the table around, rearrange and balance the foreign versus American conflict of interests.

Obtaining immigrant status is vital for the quality of life of foreigners as well as nationals because the formal registration of citizens reduces poverty and violence between the immigrant communities and Americans. It also lessens the number of undiscovered and unreported crimes.

For example, some undocumented women who suffer from domestic violence prefer not to alert the police because of the fear of being deported. Crimes committed by immigrants who lack legal presence in the United States are harder to solve and cost taxpayers more. Undocumented immigrants are allowed to pay taxes if they choose, but they are not required to do so. In most states in America immigrants without green card are not allowed to drive or work. They are also not allowed to return to the United States legally after they leave the country.

In this book I have created a system to help you succeed in your interracial relationship on American soil. Studies made in 2019 estimates that the number of undocumented immigrants living in the USA range from 10.5 million to 12 million. But this number is only what the Census Bureau's American Community Survey counts by interviewing about two million homes a year. This census asks people if they are American citizens but doesn't ask them if they are legally in the USA. Although the Department of Homeland Security (DHS) and the Department of Health and Human Services do their best to keep track of those numbers, it is known that the rate of the undocumented is much higher than that. Foreigners always keep their immigration statuses private.

At the same time I teach you how to succeed outside of American territory. This book is also for those who want to date American citizens in their own country. An Internet study this year showed that 10 million Americans are living outside of the United States. Your future American King or Queen may be located just a few miles away from your house, living in a beautiful house in Mexico City, a luxurious apartment in Rio de Janeiro or a ranch in San José. You might not need to fly to the USA yet.

This book will also help American citizens to better understand an immigrant's point of view in dating so that they can contribute to the success of their relationship or protect themselves from being the target of green card hunters. As your journey begins, you will notice that this is a radical move for the best of the dating scenario in America, and it might forever change the way you see relationships.

I divide this book into three parts. In the first part, I talk about the green card and the American dream. I introduce the strategy that I used to receive five proposals, two of which resulted in legal marriages. What's more? You will also gain a better understanding of masculinity.

In the second part, I briefly discuss femininity and how it can work to your advantage, I share techniques to attract men for those already living in the USA, and then I give specific information for immigrant women outside of the USA who want to date men in the United States.

The final part of this book discusses female stereotypes from other countries. This section is devoted to showing dating strategies for different nationalities and how to profit from negative stereotypes.

Above all else, I have tapped into my own life experiences in writing the *Green Card Chess Game* book.

# CHAPTER 1
# CASTLING ON THE KING

## WHY THE USA?

The USA, being one of the world's wealthiest countries, attracts people from all parts of the world because it cultivates the magical idea of social mobility like nowhere else. The average immigrant's dream is to exit poverty and overcome low socioeconomic status. America is welcoming and U.S. law permits many types of immigrants to cross the borders, even those that are not considered skilled or highly educated.

Most immigrants are committed to making their own dreams come true and setting the foundation of success for their children as well. Immigrants choose the USA because they know that they would have more freedom and opportunity in American territory than in their own country. While more American citizens show less patriotism and are leaving the country to find more affordable and peaceful sunset living, the immigrants are just arriving on fire, believing strongly that the USA is the place for a successful future.

## IT IS YOUR FAULT

Many American-born people do not empathize with immigrant conditions. Some insist that no one forced the immigrants to come to the USA, but does that mean all immigrants deserve everything bad that falls their way? This is not the best way to think of it for several reasons. Firstly, immigration is an activity that dates back to millions of years and an innate behavior of all natural beings. In fact, the history of all countries is also the history of immigration. Secondly, a lot of people under 18 come to the USA following their immigrating parents and they grow up without most or any of the American privileges. An immigrant child or undocumented student has no more rights to a green card than their immigrant parents.

## THE TWO SIDES OF THE COIN

On one side, there are American citizens that become targets of immigrants who only use them for the green card advantage, leading to broken hearts and, in some cases, empty pockets. On another side, there are American citizens who specifically look for immigrants with whom they can have an exploitative relationship. Those American citizens often look for beautiful young women or someone to live off financially. Some of them would have never had a chance to be with certain immigrants if it wasn't for their vulnerabilities.

## ALICE'S STORY: A CAUTIONARY TALE

I lived in Seattle, Washington, for one month in an apartment with a woman from Brazil. One day, I decided to pay a short visit to a friend in Oregon. When I came back, I tried to unlock the door, but it would not open. I called this woman I was living with, but she didn't answer her phone. Then I called her boyfriend because he was a friend of mine. I thought he could help me, but he told me, *"I'm sorry she didn't tell you, but I am moving in with her tonight."* I was desperate! I had no idea what to do or where to go.

Later, I discovered that she was jealous of the friendship between her boyfriend and me; therefore, she didn't want me around. I called my father in Orlando. He said I could stay with a friend of his while I looked for another place. He gave me the address and phone number, so I called his friend to let him know I was on my way to his house.

It took me about thirty minutes to get there. I pulled up to a huge three-story home that looked like it belonged in a movie. Outside, my dad's friend was waving to me and welcoming me to the house. After my arrival, he quickly collected two hundred dollars from me and left to go to work, so we didn't have time to talk. The house was massive, dark, and had a weird odor. It also felt cluttered.

I went to my room upstairs and put away my things. I came back downstairs to see if there was anyone else living there. Soon, a man showed up. He looked like he was in his late twenties and he was from Colombia. We chitchatted for a while. Then another man came, and he looked like he was in his late thirties. He was from Brazil. He said he rented a room in the house. Later that night, two more men arrived. I learned they were from Argentina. I had lost count of how many men lived in the house. They were all immigrants and could barely speak English. Most of them looked like they worked in construction.

Later that night, the men carried on, cracking jokes, eating, and playing Ping-Pong. It felt like I was at a party. In the middle of the socializing, a little chubby white woman with a northwestern accent arrived. She was an American in her late forties. She started cursing and throwing objects in the kitchen. She cried and asked me to forgive her for her manners.

The men acted like they had seen this behavior many times; they even looked bored. I thought she was the only American citizen that lived in the house until I saw her thirteen-year-old daughter, Kerry. Kerry and her mother stayed in their room all day. I couldn't believe it!

I wanted to make her calm down, and I was interested to know how I could help her. She told me her name was Alice. Alice asked me to come to her room. Her room looked like a completely different world compared to the rest of the house.

In tears, she told me she had married my father's friend from Brazil a year ago. She said the relationship was perfect initially, but her husband was not happy with their income.

He decided to rent their house out to all of those people that I had met earlier. She said she no longer felt comfortable or safe in her own home. She explained that was why she and her daughter hid in their room the whole day. She told me her life felt like a prison. She couldn't leave. She claimed she didn't have money because her husband controlled it all.

Alice told me she couldn't leave her immigrant husband even though they were no longer together in a relationship because he depended on her for his Green Card. As you can see from this story, a Green Card can be a prison for the immigrant and the sponsor. Both parties need to choose whom they marry wisely.

## THE BILL OF THE RELATIONSHIP

Since having lawful presence in the USA is so crucial for a sustainable life, the green card has attained a social value that transforms into a monetary value. As there's wealth in the USA, so is there poverty. It is not hard to find low in-come Americans who will gladly marry a foreigner if given a reasonable amount of money. The price of a marriage with an American citizen range between ten thousand to a hundred thousand U.S. dollars. The price varies depending on the social and economic status of the American citizen. Most immigrants believe that the better off their American spouses are, the greater their chances of having their green cards approved.

Although the law enforces the American citizen to sponsor the foreigner financially, it is pretty common to see immigrants providing full financial support to low income American citizens. Even though an immigrant is likely to get paid the least amount of money and work several hours more than the average American, it is the immigrant, not the citizen, who usually pays the bills of the relationship. It is common to see immigrant men giving their American girlfriends luxury cars, apartments and expensive gifts freely without mentioning their need for a green card. It is also common to see immigrant women living the married life, cooking, cleaning and even providing financial support to their husbands, all without important legal and government rights to themselves. If being a supportive wife is tough when you have all your rights as a citizen, imagine doing it while you don't have most of them in place.

## UNDOCUMENTED

For some people, living undocumented in the USA is better than living legally in their own home country. I have seen many people become rich after migrating to a wealthy country in North America and Europe by working in a low-status job. I have also witnessed people trying to get rich in their own country, fighting over impoverished environments, outrageous taxes, regulations, and a market with low buying potential, and failing, despite being intelligent, consistent, and committed. Your location makes a big difference in the odds of your financial success.

Living undocumented in a First-World country could mean that you will have fear and doubt about your future. You might question your worth as a productive citizen. However, many people are feeling the same way in their own home country. Living in poverty in a Third-World country means that you live in fear because of violence, crime, and government instability.

## DATING DOWN

In theory, Americans are financially responsible for their foreign spouses until they get their Green Card. There are only a few circumstances where the American citizen can terminate the obligation of support, such as in case of death or if their spouse decides to leave the USA or abandon the marriage.

However, it is common to see immigrants marrying someone with financial challenges. As an example, American spouses who can't meet the financial requirements for sponsoring an immigrant need to have another person or even many other family members do it for them.

Why do some immigrants take the end of the stick on dating? One of the many explanations is that economic migrants who are not wealthy often live in the "bad" side of town. Immigrants who are incapable of generating substantial high income connect with people with the same financial status. People who live undocumented in the USA have narrow chances of blending into high society, which is why they have a hard time finding partners who are socially and economically stable.

You don't want to be in marital relationship with a low income American citizen. Not even the U.S. government wants it. The U.S. government doesn't want immigrants using resources like welfare, Medicare, or Medicaid. The government (section 213A of the INA) can sue the sponsor for reimbursement if the immigrant receives a federal or state benefit.

## THE GREEN TABOO

A lot of women don't ask for an official marriage so that their spouses do not doubt the veracity of the relationship. Marrying only for the green card is a crime that can result in severe consequences. For this reason, there's some level of fear involved in the act of telling someone that you need the benefit, even when you have no intention of committing fraud. Marrying only for the green card is considered morally wrong and shameful. The green card is a taboo that no one likes to talk about in an international dating relationship even though it is extremely necessary. The green card subject is not a topic that people will like to speak about during a family reunion, formal gathering or work place in the presence of immigrants. In this book, I hope to break down this stigma and make people speak up about it, so no one ends up being taken advantage of.

## FRAUD

Imagine that foreigners could enter the United States as they please. If this happened, the government could no longer provide enough jobs, homes, security, and space for everyone living in the country. For this reason, marriage between a citizen and an immigrant is carefully screened for fraud.

Fraud is a marriage where the couple doesn't live in the same house or ever see each other in person or regularly. It is also called fraud when the marriage is only for the benefit status and nothing else. The USA considers the act of creating a fraudulent marriage a serious crime that can get an immigrant deported and banned from the States.

## THE GOVERNMENT OF MARRIAGE

The rate of success in marriages is a great concern to the U.S. government. The government wants to ensure that the union will last and for this to happen the couple needs to appear compatible. They consider the age difference of the couple. A wide age gap wouldn't stop you from getting your green card, but it may raise red flags. Kerry Abrams, associate professor of law and co-director of the University of Virginia School of Law's Center for Children, Families and the Law, published a paper in 2007 called, *Immigration*

*Law and the Regulation of Marriage.'* In it she discusses how immigration law regulates courtship:

> *Immigration law regulates courtship through the use of so-called fiancé or K-1 visas. A fiancé visa allows an immigrant to enter the United States for up to ninety days for the purpose of marrying a U.S. citizen. Fiancé visas allow cross-national couples to marry within the United States and also provide a means for couples who intend to marry but need more courtship time in the same geographic location together.*

In her paper, she also states that a Fiancé visa will only be approved if the couple has previously met in person within two years before the date of filing the petition. The couple has to have a bona-fide intention to marry and be legally able and willing to conclude a valid marriage in the United States within ninety days after the alien's arrival.

In a traditional marriage, couples can choose not to engage in sexual intercourse or share the same bed, and they can even live in separate houses without being questioned. However, marriage between an immigrant and a citizen needs to be traditional. The reason is that America believes that traditional marriage can bring order to society through family ties. She says that by interfering in marriage, immigration law regulates the family more than protects American borders. For example, many years ago, the government wouldn't give immigrant benefits to those entering same-sex marriage. It also expects an immigrant's marriage to be more successful. Harmful behaviors such as alcoholism, verbal abuse, poverty, incarceration, and mental health issues can be reasons for an immigrant to be denied citizenship.

## APPLYING FOR A GREEN CARD

There are two main types of visas for entering the United States: *nonimmigrant visas* and *immigrant visas*. A nonimmigrant visa is for foreigners who intend to stay in America temporarily. For example, they come for tourism, medical treatment, business meetings, education, etc. On the other hand, an immigrant visa allows you to permanently live in America, but this is not an easy process because it is only available for the highly educated, those with extraordinary ability, and an American citizen's direct relatives.

Be aware that marrying a citizen of the United States will not automatically give you immigration status. You have to apply for the benefit. Most states require the couple to get a marriage license. After the marriage paperwork is complete, the court will send the certificate to the couple's address in less than a week.

You can start the Green Card process even before you receive the marriage certificate. First, you will need a copy of your passport or photo ID and a copy of your I-94, if it is still valid. You'll need a birth certificate translated into English. If you have been married before, a divorce or death certificate of the other partner is required. Two passport photos and medical exams Performed by a United States Citizenship and Immigration Services (USCIS)-approved medical doctor are needed. Also, your name needs to be on the lease. It would be best to have joint bank accounts, shared health insurance, and anything else that proves a bona-fide marriage.

There is around $1,000 in USCIS filing fee, but you can get it waived in some cases if you have a financial hardship. You can hire a lawyer to submit the paperwork, or you can do it yourself. The forms are available to download online.

The time and process will depend on various things such as whether you have entered the United States legally or illegally. If you enter illegally, it will take more bureaucratic steps and more time. States where there are less immigrants are faster compared to states where there are more immigrants. The northern part of the United States is more immigrant friendly and supports the presence of foreigners more than the south, therefore the northern wait is shorter. The time is longer if your spouse is a green card holder other than an American citizen. If you apply within the United States it is faster, but if applying from outside of the country it is a longer wait. After you fill out the forms, submit them to your state's USCIS facility. When they receive your documents, they will mail you a form called I-797C, which is a notice of the action that the USCIS is working on your case.

A few months later, you will receive a letter with an appointment to have your biometrics taken. After that, if you have also requested it together with the green card, you will obtain your work permit and a SSN valid for work only. Then you will receive an appointment for your Green Card interview. You will receive your Green Card no more than 120 days after the interview. If you are denied you still have a chance to retry. If it doesn't work the first time, the immigration is not likely to give you a deportation letter, and in most cases you can keep trying. After you have your Green Card, you can remove the conditions and become a permanent U.S. citizen.

## THE ANATOMY OF THE RELATIONSHIP

When a relationship begins, both man and woman are on their best behavior. Many people call it the honeymoon phase. During this period, the couple typically doesn't argue. The sexual attraction is strong, and both people are well groomed, perfumed, dressed to impress, and talk sweetly to each other.

After the honeymoon phase is over and the couple has become comfortable with each other, they both begin to reveal the aspects of themselves that they had suppressed. Little things about each other start to become a problem. It's hard to stand the noise when they chew their food, or the way they drag their feet when they walk, or their lack of cleanliness. Many couples hold onto the memories from the beginning of the relationship, and they stay in it expecting that their partner will go back to being Miss Docile or Mr. Right again.

## CHOOSING YOUR ROLE

The first thing to do when you are entering a relationship is to define if you will be feminine or masculine. I advise women and gay men looking for love and a Green Card to choose the feminine side. By selecting the feminine, you will play the role of the receiver. In your relationship, the masculine and feminine roles need to be clearly defined. There must be balance. There can't be two masculine roles or two feminine roles. If you choose to be feminine, your feelings will be cherished, and if you are masculine, your thinking will be respected. When there's an exchange of masculine and feminine giving, both will receive what they want.

There are men that are good at providing emotional support for their women, but are not skilled at providing financial support. There are also men that are only good at providing financially and will never acknowledge or understand your desires. If this is the type of man you choose, he won't cherish your feelings and emotions, and you will probably have to cherish his thinking and his emotions at the same time. Most people would categorize the second scenario as a toxic relationship.

## ANDRÉ THE ANDROGEN

I have been in relationships where I had to cherish not only the ideas of my partners, but also their feelings. Was it toxic? It was not toxic, but it was unfulfilling.

Years ago I was in a relationship with a man much older than me who was very difficult to deal with because he was so in tune with his feminine side. What do I mean by that? He was not being masculine when he was more preoccupied in making himself happy than in making me happy. He wanted me to listen to him for hours and cherish his feelings. But he still kept the "benefit" of the masculine side by having me validate his thinking and trust his leadership. I didn't get to express my negative emotions in a safe way without being punished. I felt prohibited from being a woman and forced to fake a feminine frame that he didn't deserve to experience. I would talk sweet, smile, ask questions, use a seductive baby voice and never confront him. I felt terrible.

If a man attempts to neglect, mistreat, or control you in a toxic way, stand up for yourself immediately. You must correct his behavior at the exact moment when it happens. Address the situation directly and don't hold a grudge. It is unattractive to hold on to grudges and look sad around the house. Don't wait for him to ask you what made you upset. If you love yourself, you should not be afraid to protect your feelings. Let me caution you. Do not raise your voice or yell while speaking up. You must do it in a way that sounds elegant, effortless, and pain-free. Remember, you are the prize. Protecting and standing up for yourself is your hobby.

## WHAT HOLDS A RELATIONSHIP TOGETHER?

Sex alone will not make a relationship last long-term. You must create agreements about who is in charge of the finances, the shopping, paying the bills, cooking, cleaning, and household maintenance. There needs to be a clear and open conversation about private property and what belongs to whom. Without clear rules, one partner will likely give more than the other, which can create resentment. If the roles and responsibilities are not clear, one partner may feel like they were seduced by guilt and manipulation.

Compromises have to be made in a relationship. A woman will allow the man to be the financial provider, and the man will commit to monogamy. As a woman, the safest thing to do is pretend to be dependent on a man financially while having your own side business or investment without his notice. Don't let him notice how much money you have because he wants to rescue you and take care of you. Men fall in love when they give, and the more they give, the deeper they will love.

# CHAPTER 2
# QUEENS DON'T GIVE IT UP

## NO MARRIAGE, NO SEX

If you apply all the techniques that I teach you in this book in your relationship but don't follow the piece of advice I am about to give you, everything you work for will go to waste. The important piece of advice I have for you is never having sex with a man before he has married you. Most of the relationship coaches will tell you that you don't need to go that far. They would tell you that time invested and a verbal commitment is enough. However I disagree completely! You would be impressed about how fast you can take a man to the altar if you don't have any kind of sex with him. In this day and age, making a man wait for sex seems like an impossible task. But once you master the ability to think strategically and have unshakable standards, you can do it. Waiting to have sex is easy, not just for you but for the other party as well and that is how I got married the first time six months after meeting my ex-husband. It is also how I got married four months after meeting my second husband and was proposed to by three other men.

How are you going to do that? You are going to become a great negotiator. Dr. Pat Allen, a licensed MFT and certified cognitive behavioral therapist and transactional analyst with a practice spanning over thirty years, teaches that there are three forms of getting what you want from people: command, seduction, or negotiation:

> *The first form, command or intimidation, happens when someone threatens to hurt others if they don't do what was requested. Seduction is when someone uses mind games to get others to do what they want. Seduction can awakens feelings of guilt, shame and other lower levels of thinking in the person who is being convinced to act a certain way. But it can be a positive thing depending how you use it. However, a lot of women use seduction with guilt and shame to get what they want. What do they do? They give up sex first and ask for a commitment later. They attempt to seduce with guilt. But men take the chance of casual sex without any remorse. Women then end up feeling used. The third way is by negotiation and is the best way to get what you want. That*

*is how you will get any man to commit to you
entirely on your terms without feeling used.*

## JENNIFER'S GREEN CARD

Jennifer was a beautiful woman born in France. At a young age, she was abandoned by her parents and left in an orphanage. She grew up to be a talented dressmaker. By the age of eighteen, she gained many followers on social media by posting pictures of her work. A big company in the evening- and wedding-dress industry sponsored her work visa to come to the United States.

In the USA, she met her first husband, John, at an evening gala event for her company. Jennifer was instantly attracted to him. John was a perfect gentleman and proposed to her in less than a year. Unfortunately, right after they got married, he became physically and verbally abusive towards her. Jennifer decided to divorce John and didn't apply for her Green Card because she wanted to leave the relationship as soon as possible.

A year later, she met another man named Matt whom she thought was a perfect match. He was ten years older and had a career in the medical field. After they got married, she discovered he was cheating on her the whole time they were together. Jennifer divorced for a second time without applying for her Green Card because, again, she didn't want to stay in the relationship.

Soon after, she met Kurt who was a member of the gym where she exercised. Kurt was twenty years older than her. He was in real estate and had his financial life together. At the same time, Jennifer and I became friends when I met her while shopping at the store where she worked. She told me she was so comfortable with Kurt and was falling for him quickly. I told her to be careful not to engage in intimacy with Kurt until he committed to her. I told her she required a promise ring and a commitment from Kurt to take care of her, provide for her financially, and be faithful to her. Kurt agreed, but with the condition that she move in with him. Jennifer let him know that she required being married first.

Kurt acted differently than all the men Jennifer had dated, and within a few months, he proposed to her. Jennifer started to love her new life, and all she wanted to do was spend time with her husband, being a housewife. If she chose to leave her job as a designer, she would have lost her work visa. Kurt sponsored Jennifer to get her Green Card, and they lived happily for years.

Later, Jennifer got divorced from Kurt, but they remain friends. She considers him as her family. Jennifer opened up a wedding dress shop and she does well financially as a designer.

## FRANK'S STORY

Frank was a Colombian gay man on an extended tourist visa in the United States. He was living in Texas for almost a year before meeting his future husband. Frank had to return to his home country soon because his visa was expiring.

At that time, Frank was a handsome, twenty-year-old feminine man who loved wearing tight shorts that showed off his muscular legs. On the day he met Christopher, he was wearing an open-collared floral shirt with a gold necklace and gold rings on each of his hands. As Frank waited for his coffee at a coffee shop, a man passed by and bumped his shoulder.

The man intended to get Frank to move out of his way by purposely hitting him slightly. Frank had already experienced the same hatred from some straight men who disagreed with his lifestyle. Before Frank responded, another man came to Frank's rescue. A masculine gay man named Christopher approached Frank, and he asked if that guy was bothering him. Frank smiled and said, *"Everything is good now that you are here to help."* Christopher smiled back at Frank, and they spent the next hour talking and getting to know each other.

As the relationship progressed over the next few weeks, they became a couple and lived together. Frank was playing the role of a house boyfriend. I spent time with Frank, and he expressed that he was sad. He wanted to stay with Christopher, but he had to return to Colombia because his visa was expiring. I suggested that Frank marry Christopher, but he said it was too soon for Christopher to make such a big decision. I told him that if it was too fast for Christopher, they should not live together. I suggested to Frank that he move out of his boyfriend's house. I asked him what the point of getting married was if his boyfriend was already reaping the benefits of the marriage.

If Frank wanted to become Christopher's husband, he would need to stop giving husband benefits without a commitment. Frank moved out, and they still lived close but in separate houses. The distance didn't make Christopher propose right away. It took a few months until he was convinced. Frank was almost on his way back to Colombia when Christopher proposed marriage to him in the airport. The ceremony happened less than a month after the proposal. Christopher had the wedding at his house. About forty people attended the event, including me. Frank moved back into Christopher's home, and they have been happy ever since then.

# CHAPTER 3
# MEN AND SEX

The best way to win a chess match is by predicting your adversary's next move before he can predict yours. When it comes to dating, you have to understand men at such a deep level that you can anticipate their actions before they make sense of what you are planning.

You should never waste time. If you rush into a relationship with a man without first uncovering who he is, you can face challenges later in the relationship. On the other hand, if the relationship progresses too slowly, another woman may catch his eye, and you will still lose. To win the game, you may have to make tough choices and sacrifices along the way. There needs to be a mixture between your feelings and your rational self.

## WHAT NOT TO SAY TO A MAN
One of the biggest mistakes I made in my past relationships was speaking up loud and proud to a man that I would not have sex with him unless I was married. It was a mistake because it made me appear too demanding and

bossy. Stating this too boldly up front called attention to the man's sex agenda and hurt his ego. Also most men would never come to the table if they knew that would be no sex involved in the first place. Every masculine man desires the companionship of a sensual, sexy, and feminine woman by his side. He wants a woman who has luscious goodies and homemaking skills, but above all, he wants someone who can give him sex.

Another mistake was to mention marriage before they had even asked me for sex. Instead of asserting authority, the best thing to do is ask for a commitment as soon as he asks you for sex. If that doesn't work, it is best to disappear without breaking up with him. You can tell him you love him but are confused about where the relationship is going. He will most likely be willing to commit once you take yourself away from his sight. Don't break up with him because it will lead to a permanent scar on the relationship, which could be impossible to repair.

Another mistake I made was telling a man that I was setting a schedule for when I would provide sex for him. I did that with my ex-boyfriend. I told him I would only have sex with him once every two weeks. He got really mad. *"This is insane, I'm never obeying your demands!"* Two weeks passed by and he came over and asked me for sex again. I said: *"I'm not in a mood."* His reply: *"But you said two weeks!"* So make your own sexual contract and do not tell him the terms and conditions.

Men are smart problem solvers that want to satisfy women's deepest desires. What is a man's job in a relationship? A man's job is to uplift a woman, to provide, protect, and comfort her so that she can feel safe to be her most authentic self. As Dr. John Grays puts out, a man needs to do the job and a woman needs someone to do the job. A man wants to fulfill feelings of significance and make the relationship feel purposeful. Men want to feel successful in the task of making their woman happier.

The male side of the relationship is in charge of the material aspect of it. The man works, brings income to the household, and pays the bills. A masculine man wants to protect, give, and cherish the feelings of his woman. He wants to know how you feel about the decisions he makes. A woman brings balance to his masculinity, and then he feels safe to be vulnerable and open up his sensitive side. Men are programmed to be tough and hold back their emotions, but women can create the stability and safety for men to be themselves. A man will never be fully happy without a woman in his life and home. Marriage unleashes the good in him.

Men are better when they are married. I believe most men want to get married. They love the idea of being the man of the house. His quality of life increases, he eats healthier, he works harder, he becomes more cherishing. Marriage gives a man status. Marriage gives the perception that he is desirable.

In romantic relationships, intimacy is closeness, familiarity, and rapport. Intimacy grows when you nurture feelings with someone you trust. You engage in long conversations and share your thoughts and deepest secrets. When there is mutual trust, it leads to a commitment. When there is deep trust and commitment, you allow your partner to share more of your body. You kiss, embrace, and let your partner see more of your skin. You give and receive massages to each other.

Intimacy grows on a physical level, but do not engage in sex until after marriage. Your body is sacred. Don't give a man wife privileges if you are only a girlfriend. He doesn't get to sleep in your bed, even if you are not having sex. Once you are engaged, you can open yourself to what you feel comfortable with, but hold off on oral sex and intercourse until after marriage when you are fully open to give and receive.

So you need a commitment before sex. Why do you need a commitment? It is because men bond when they earn a woman's love, and men also bond through the commitments that they make, not through sex. Get a real commitment before you hand over your amazing gifts! Don't move in with him and play the role of a wife at all if he hasn't married you. They will not fall in love with you if you don't get them to commit.

In addition, for masculine men, romance means fantasizing that a woman trusts his leadership, listens to his ideas, and respects him. A masculine man falls in love when he gives, protects, provides, and takes care of a woman. A masculine man bonds when he keeps the commitments he makes. A man does not commit in exchange for sex. Commitment must precede sex every time.

Dr. Pat Allen teaches in her books and seminars that a man projects a virtuous image on the woman he wants to marry. That way, he falls in love with the part of the woman's brain who cannot have casual sex or move forward in the relationship without an engagement. *"Masculine men know that there are no free lunches, and what appears to be free sex usually has strings attached—strings being a woman who either says, 'Marry me,' or 'I'm pregnant,' or 'I feel used.' Men will always accept free sex, but then run away without taking care of the bill, leaving a woman bonded and in pain."*

According to my own experience, not providing sex to a man will make him obsessed with you. He will want to marry you in less than three months. Why do you want to marry that fast? It's because there's absolutely no reason to wait and because time is an illusion. People are also not getting any younger. When it comes to a woman's time, the best thing to do is not waste a second. After they get married is when they fall in love.

Believe that your man wants to make all your wishes come true and if you prefer to wait until you get married or until you get your green card to have sex with him, so be it. I don't believe that sex is so important that it defines the veracity of a relationship. I see people who stop having sex with each other after only five years of being together and old couples who no longer have sex but are still in love. Put your needs first because deep inside that's what all men want more than sex. I don't advise women to have any kind of romantic relationship with men whom they are not genuinely physically attracted to.

Be aware that men desire sex. Why do men have a voracious hunger for sex? Men, like women, have a fundamental desire for connection. Having sex is how a man connects to a woman. Men also need sex to regulate their hormones, which is essential to maintain a healthy body. Nature has put men in charge of the number of replications of our species, but not the quality. Although their hearts are programmed for love, their bodies are designed for cold and selfish sex. Biologically men want to have as much sex as they can, so that nature can maximize genetic success. Men have a natural talent for using mind games and charming personalities to deceive women to fall for their tricks and give them sex.

No one else will tell you, so I will. Men make money, go to college, and work hard to be good enough to have sex with women. They are obsessed with vaginas. They want to penetrate them orally, with their fingers, their penis, and anything else they can find. It's what they think about all day.

I spent my teenage years thinking that only a fraction of men were ultra-sexual. If that was true, every time we told a man that we wouldn't provide sex, they would stick around! On this journey I have been stood up, ghosted, blocked, cursed and mocked by men who could not accept my standards. Men who thought they were so entitled to sex that they had the right to be furious about a woman's boundaries. Only a few men will be willing to wait until marriage to have sex. Even fewer will accept to wait until you receive your Green Card to have sex. As I already said, if sex wasn't on the table, most men would never come to the table in the first place.

What can you do? Seek only for a masculine man. Men on their masculine energy are willing to wait for sex. Studies have shown that the less sex a man gets, and the less he masturbates, the more his testosterone rises up and the more he wants to please women.

If you provide sex to a man without a commitment, he is very likely to completely vanish afterwards. This is because men change after they get what they want from you. Inside every moral and ethical man, there's another insensitive, apathetic, and stressed one waiting to emerge. The first man shows up before a woman has sex with him. He is on his best behavior. He's sweet and a good listener. The second man shows up after a woman has sex with him without a commitment. This man is less communicative, always busy, and isn't there to meet your needs any longer.

According to Dr. John Gray, author of the book *Men Are from Mars, Women Are from Venus,* it's true that men change after sex. The reason for that is because after they ejaculate, they receive a great dose of oxytocin, a female hormone, which lowers his testosterone. With oxytocin in his body, he is stressed out and uncomfortable. He needs time and space to recharge his body with testosterone so that he can feel good again. So they leave, but they will come back.

According to my experience, a man will never ghost a highly sexually attractive woman after sex no matter how soon she had sex with him. He doesn't want to lose this beauty asset, and he will keep her in his radar as long as she still looks sexy. Many extremely attractive sex workers have said that if they don't set a timer for their clients to work with, they would never leave.

A man wants to have sex with an attractive woman more than once and that's why he plays unavailability games after sex because he is afraid she will lose interest. A man can also give a woman an unexpected large gift or a big sum of money and disappear because he has fantasies of being chased by women. Notice that in all of those scenarios men are also feeding their desire for sex or their ego. If you don't follow my advice and hold off from having sex, you will likely have to start all over with a new man. It means that casual sex will almost never lead to a real loving and committed relationship.

What if a hook up turns into a commitment? There's a small chance that you can win the Green Card Chess Game by providing sex to a man sooner than later. In fact, a lot of gold diggers win the heart of top millionaires by giving it up after only three days of dating and some even a few hours after meeting for the first time. A lot of those women do not require any amount of money or gifts upfront from those men that they sleep with. In fact, they refuse to disclose any interest in money, fine dining, lifestyle and economic class ascendency. They refuse to receive money or gifts and many of them even pay on dates. They present themselves as being humble entrepreneurs, social workers, philanthropists and even highly religious. But notice that these women are very smart and they use their own strategy.

This strategy consists of making a man feel sexually desirable and wanted, not for what they can do or what they can give to a woman, but for who they are. The idea that a woman reveals genuine attraction towards them drives men into insatiable passion. It is the feeling that she is not playing any games and everything happened "naturally." They prefer to marry a woman who has never asked them for a penny, even if that is because she has low self-esteem. Most of them are repulsed by gold diggers. Some men are deeply bothered by the idea of a woman wanting their money that they prefer to overlook many of the facts. Some overlook the fact that if she slept with him too soon, some other man did. Some overlook the fact that if he didn't have to do anything, some other man didn't neither. This is because some wealthy men tend to have big egos. They won't accept that they are not unique or special and their women would have settled for anything else. That's how those women get large sums of money from men and marriage proposals.

This strategy is a very bold move. I'm intrigued by their ability to detach, to have casual sex without feeling hurt in case their plan doesn't work out. But if it works, he will never doubt the relationship.

In reality, a man will never know for sure if a woman has ulterior motives for being with him. It doesn't matter if you make him wait, make him pay or don't ask for anything. The same way, he will never know if you only had good intentions and never planned to take advantage of him. I have been mistaken for a gold digger and a green card hunter many times. Although I had only good intentions, I had poor delivery. That's why you have to get into a man's feelings no matter what your intentions are. This is because when a man falls in love he becomes completely blind to any of those "details." When you win a man's heart, you win the Green Card Chess Game.

## MARRYING OLDER MEN

Older men and younger women are a great match for each other. According to Dr. Pat Allen, young women and older men bond because they're driven by estrogen. Young men and older women don't bond because they are driven by testosterone and progesterone. In the United States, the age group with the highest income are those at 65 and upwards.

Therefore, if you choose to date an older man, you are more likely to experience better quality of life.

However, in my experience, the age gap must not be too wide because it is extremely difficult to take a man to the altar when he is much older than you, especially if he is very wealthy. There are two main reasons for that. Firstly because dating and mating a man much older than you will make you look like one of those scammers who prey on the elderly and vulnerable. Therefore, his friends with whom he cultivates a solid relationship, starting some many years before you were born, will sabotage your marriage. Secondly because a man can be sexually attracted to a woman's body, but have no connection to her mind. If a man can't connect with a woman's inner world and inner feelings, she will not be happy. A lot of older men do not care if there's absolutely no connection between the very young woman they are with and themselves. They are there for the sex only.

Some men who are much older will behave like their father or grandfather, but lust after them like after any other ordinary woman. There's nothing they can do to fix this because, in reality, he could actually be their father or grandfather. They are not doing anything wrong and no one chooses how old they are.

Men can easily deal with a parental relationship as long as they get to look at a beautiful young woman every day. However, a parental relationship will make any woman miserable. This situation actually happened to me many times over. I got into relationships with men that were much older and I became their child. This kind of relationship is easy to maintain because it creates an addicting, dependence pattern for the giver that is hard to break. Also, on those parental relationships you receive a lot without needing to give anything in return. Although the parental relationship seems like a paradise, it will never make a woman happy. Eventually a woman will feel alone and wish for a man, for romance, not a father. A real relationship is when he is her man and she is his woman. You don't need to marry a man much older than you to get him to meet all your needs. You don't need to engage in relationships with men who are extremely physically unattractive in your opinion.

## UGLY MEN

I take myself as an example because I wasted much of my time dating men who were out of my league physically. I wrongly thought ugly men could give me more in a relation-ship. I thought I was choosing the easier path. However, it never worked out well for me. Firstly because a man who is extremely unattractive compared to you will never trust you since he thinks you have ulterior motives for dating him in the first place. Secondly because they don't want to take you seriously since they believe they can't maintain the relationship. They think they could have you for one night, but could not afford or do not possess the confidence to handle a long term relationship with you. I have been on dates with those kinds of men. They would take the time to touch my leg under the table and invade my personal boundaries. By the end of dinner they would always solicit me, ask me how much to go to the hotel with them or make me an offer in cash. Those dates only made me feel hurt.

## YOUNG, RICH AND HANDSOME

I would say that young, rich and handsome sometimes are the biggest ballers. When it comes to marriage, they are pretty naive. That's why it is a lot easier to convince a young man in his early twenties to marry you than a man in his late fifties. Young men are excited with the idea of being the provider and protector of the household. It is a window for them to grow up and they love the feeling of adventure that it brings. They will not assume that you have ulterior motives, especially if they are very handsome.

During my journey I realized that young, wealthy and handsome men were easier choices than old, ugly or obese men. However, marrying the young, rich and handsome has a price. Younger men have a much stronger sex drive than older men. Younger men will not be content with chitchatting, naked cuddling or oral sex. They want the sex Hollywood promised them, sometimes even more than once a day. For me, I could never keep up with their sex drive, and I'd rather perform less in the bedroom. Remember that everything that is abundant loses its value over time. Some handsome men are okay with waiting for sex before marriage. Maybe they have no reason to be impatient because they could get it easily from someone else.

I have always dated older and unattractive men and I didn't have to do much to keep them around. I didn't even have to have sex with most of them, which made the relationship feel more innocent, less demanding, and kept my power intact. You choose what you value the most. I always felt happier that way. But now, my priorities have changed. I have become tired of being in relationships with men I'm not attracted to.

If you find the right man, no matter if he is ugly, handsome, old or young, he will give you the world to have you on his arm. What is handsome for one person might not be so for another.

CHAPTER 4

# CASTLING ON THE QUEEN

## WHAT IT MEANS TO BE FEMININE

Femininity is a set of attributes, roles, and behaviors associated with biological or nonbiological-born females. Dr. Pat Allen teaches that feminine women bring sensuality to relationships and a feminine woman is in charge of the abstract aspect. She is consistently sweet, affectionate, kind, and loving.

Feminine woman are appreciative for what they have. A feminine woman is open to receive from all sources in nature, including her partner. A feminine woman is expected to sound good, taste good, and smell good. Feminine women should cherish the thoughts of the masculine side of the relationship.

For a feminine woman, intimacy and romance are two separate things. According to Pat Allen, to a feminine woman romance means fantasizing that a man cares so much about her that he is responsible for her feelings. He is also willing to do anything to guarantee that she is happy. Intimacy is not only when she has intercourse with a man but also when she talks, listens, touches, and smells him.

> *"Many women allow the intimacy of intercourse when what they really want are strokes of friendly affection — tender loving care (TLC). One of the big promotional abuses in the world today is telling women that they can experience intimate intercourse indiscriminately without hurting themselves. Since women are feel- thinkers and need to be safe and trusting for true sexual surrender, a woman who either invites or allows fast sex runs the risk of desensitizing herself to a total orgasmic experience."*

## THE FEMININE ROLE

The role of a feminine woman is to make the house feel like a home. Your feminine presence should be felt not only on a physical level but as an essence throughout the home, a spiritual sanctuary. Allow your man to do masculine acts like taking care of you, being the protector, and to provide for you financially. In turn, as a feminine woman, you should take care of yourself by eating healthily, exercising, styling your hair, and doing your makeup. You should also dress in a feminine and sensual way. After you accomplish those things, all you have to do is smile and seduce a man with your eyes. You won't need to say anything.

When you present yourself as being a feminine woman, a man wants to take care of you. All the goodness inside of them is suddenly unlocked. When a gay man comes off as being feminine, he also gets the same kind of responses from a masculine gay man.

## SUPER FEMININE

If a woman is overly feminine, she takes care of a grown man as if he were her child. She cleans and cooks for him. Some women would never serve a fried egg with a broken yolk to her man but would eat that one herself. Some women serve their man first before serving their kids.

There needs to be balance in your femininity, so be sure not to over-feminize yourself to the point where you are unnecessarily submissive. A man is not your boss if he is not your husband.

## MASCULINE WOMAN

Overly masculine women may curse, overeat, and be physically or verbally aggressive. Masculine women do not take the time to show appreciation for what they have accomplished or their level of success. There's no amount of money that can satisfy a masculine woman. They want more money, more houses, more cars... They don't verbalize appreciation even when they feel it. A masculine woman can also be hateful towards man.

One common behavior of a masculine woman is to initiate sex. Masculine women seek the pleasure of intercourse and not affection or lovemaking. They refuse to receive compensation for sex, and they may become offended when a man offers to give them money or gifts. An overly masculine woman will not receive gifts, trips, cars, and diamonds. They only get casual, cold, penetrating sex from a man. Men don't fall in love with that type of woman. In the book, *Getting to "I Do,"* by Patricia Allen, she says, *"Having penetrating, controlling, passionate intercourse is very male in energy. Making total love, physically, mentally, and emotionally, is very feminine and affection-based."*

If you have too much masculine energy, you will not attract a commitment from a man. Giving up sex too easily ruins your chances. As I have said throughout the book, attracting and keeping a man long-term comes from not giving sex away for free. A man needs to earn and prove that he deserves access to your body through a commitment.

## THE FEMININE AND MASCULINE
Femininity relates to masculinity when there is a negotiation and trade of commodities and goods. The exchange of assets consists of the male partner being the provider of material things and the female providing the relationship's abstract aspect. Men and women have their roles and contribute in different ways. The masculine energy provides and protects, while the feminine energy takes care of the emotions and

feelings. The feminine role leads covertly while letting the masculine role feel in charge.

Feminine women can successfully relate to men by taking care of their appearance. Men are stimulated visually. A man sees a woman as a sex object first, so use it to your advantage when attracting a man. Show off your curves and cleavage. Watch your diet and take good care of your body.

## THE SCAM

A man who treated me very well, took me on romantic dinners and bought me gifts married me within four months after meeting for the first time. But he changed completely after marriage. He accused me of being with him just for the green card, he refused to sign the paperwork for citizenship. He even pretended he was mentally incapable of signing it. One week later, I grabbed all my belongings and moved back to my father's house. I filed for the divorce myself and didn't apply for my green card.

The lesson I want you to learn from my story is that you should never marry a man whom you don't know enough about. Another lesson is to run away from any man that accuses you of being with them only for the green card. Even if he said such a thing just one time during a small disagreement. Especially be aware even if he jokes about it. Those types of men will delay your green card process. They can get you deported or mess up your green card interview, causing you to lose the benefit. They will continue to torment you because deep down they believe they have nothing else to offer you except a green card. Those types of men are way out of your league and following them means their low self-esteem will sabotage your dreams.

## HE CAN'T CUT IT!

Almost five months into a relationship with a sixty-three-year-old man I was dating from Kansas, I became impatient about waiting for a proposal. I had already asked him who would change his diapers when he was no longer able to do it for himself. I bought sexy lingerie and wore it around the house, but I told him that only my husband was allowed to take it off me! I didn't get the response I was seeking from him and he didn't appear to care.

If the man you are dating won't propose, you may have to use psychology. In this situation, I was willing to challenge him because I wasn't getting what I wanted. If he wasn't ready to propose, then I wasn't going to waste any more of my time in this relationship.

Psychological techniques can be helpful with getting a proposal sooner. First, let the man know how important marriage is to you because it shows a sign of commitment and how much he cares about you. He needs to know what will make you happy. Men feel good when they know they can make their woman happy. If you don't see him making an effort to move forward, you can shock him by talking about making a significant change in your life. You might tell him you want to move to a different state or pursue a job somewhere else. Show him other apartments that you are looking at if you move. This lets him know that you are willing to leave him if he doesn't propose. Be willing to listen to his fears about getting married so you can reassure him that life will only get better, especially because then you will be open to a sexual relationship.

## DANGER

As you enter the dating arena, always protect yourself before you make a new move. Watch out for men with predatory personalities. There are situations where men take advantage of foreign women. They assert power over the women because they are financially responsible for them and control their benefit of citizenship.

In an extreme example, two mail-order Russian brides were murdered in 1995 and 2003. If you are undocumented, you have a higher risk of facing abuse because the American citizen can threaten you with deportation. If you have children with the citizen, you can face the threat of losing or being separated from them.

Immigration law gives U.S. citizens the responsibility to petition for the green card of their spouses. There are cases where the U.S. citizen mistreats their spouse and prevents them from acquiring immigrant status. If an immigrant suffers cruelty at the hand of a citizen, they receive the right to petition for a green card for themselves under the

Violence Against Women Act (VAWA), and its objective is to release control over their immigration status without the spouse's assistance.

## TYPICAL DANGEROUS MEN

In the book *How to Spot a Dangerous Man Before You Get Involved,* author Sandra L. Brown describes eight types of dangerous men. All of these types of men are a potential risk for your mental and physical health. Often, a dangerous man has been abused by his parents growing up and will then afflict abuse in some form on a woman.

Brown identifies the eight types of dangerous men as:

1. *The Permanent Clinger:* He's needy and drains your energy.

2. *The Parental Seeker:* He wants you to take care of him and play the role of a parent.

3. *The Emotionally Unavailable Man:* He makes you feel like you are never enough, and may be committed to someone else.

4. *The Man with the Hidden Life:* He hides secrets from you and makes you feel paranoid.

5. *The Mentally Ill Man:* He has a mental illness.

6. *The Addict:* He has any kind of addiction.

7. *The Abusive or Violent Man:* He is physically, emotionally, and/or sexually abusive.

8. *The Emotional Predator:* He torments a vulnerable woman in some way.

If you encounter this type of person, leave the relationship as soon as you see or experience the man's abusive nature.

## IRINA'S STORY

Irina was a twenty-four-year-old woman from Moldova when she first came to the USA for a visit. She met Alejandro, a Panamanian American who was twenty-seven. She felt extremely attracted to him at first sight. Alejandro was a prince to Irina. There was never a thing that he would not do for her. Irina felt so blessed for having such a great man in her life.

Soon Alejandro turned into her first boyfriend, and a few months later, he became her husband. The first months of marriage went smoothly, and they both were happy. However, about a year later, Irina found out through social media that Alejandro was cheating on her. Irina was so in love with him that she accepted Alejandro's apologies and decided not to break off the relationship. But Alejandro didn't stop cheating on her.

Irina found out that he was with many other women as well. Alejandro started to steal money from her to sustain his multiple relationships. He took her car and crashed it. He received a DUI and she did not get any insurance money because her husband was driving under the influence of alcohol. Without money and a car, she kept working at her supermarket cashier job and depended on rides from coworkers.

Irina did not stop loving Alejandro, even though he had betrayed her in many ways. She continued in the relationship until Alejandro started to hit her physically. After he'd hit her on several occasions, she decided to leave the relationship. Unfortunately she hadn't gotten her Green Card yet. Irina's lawyer advised her to apply for a benefit under VAWA. This act was created in 1994, and one of its purposes is to provide immigration relief through a process of *self-petition*. It means immigrant women who are victims of domestic violence can battle for immigrant benefits independently without their violent partner's sponsorship.

## JUST FOR THE GREEN CARD

Your home is your sanctuary, and sharing your life with a man you are repulsed by will make you miserable. It doesn't matter how much money he has or how good he treats you, if you don't love him, life will be a burden of discomfort.

No matter how big the house is, there will be never enough square feet to give you space. Despite how infrequently you will have to see your husband, you will feel suffocated. It is not worth the chase to marry someone just for the green card or just for money. I doubt that you can withstand such a sad life for long.

## PAMPERED PAMELA

Pamela was from Uruguay and she married just for the green card. She got her man to marry her in the same month that they met. Pamela required several provisions and protections from her husband. He was required to pay all the bills and provide all her needs while she didn't need to do anything.

Pamela was treated like a princess and her husband was like a slave to her. There was nothing she requested that he wouldn't do for her immediately. Nonetheless she felt miserable. The house felt like a funeral. She had no drive to go out, to travel or do anything with her husband. No matter how good he was to her, how generous, loving and respectful, she only felt repulse and increasing resentment every day.

It was the longest two years of her life. By the end of her green card process, Pamela was feeling so broken inside and so unhappy that she spent double of the time in therapy to due to the severe depression she fell into.

# CHAPTER 5

# MONEY IS NOT EVERYTHING

The more a man spends money on you, the greater he sees your value. Spending money on you strokes his emotional ego. So the more he spends, the more he loves you. You become an investment and therefore a valuable asset. Men get attached to their investments, so they will be less likely to walk away from the relationship.

However, don't ask a man for money. The best way to get a man to spend on you is by not asking him for anything. I am not saying that you should give it all up in the hope that one day he'd finally decide to appreciate your efforts. All I'm saying is that you should take yourself out of a man's sight who is not spending freely. If they are not spending, just leave. But leave for good, not just to manipulate them. Find a new man who will give you freely without you having to ask for anything. Men have fantasies about coming to the rescue of a beautiful woman who will not ask them for anything. Those same men expect sex and attention from women without giving them anything either. Don't give to a man before he gives you first. Remember that if he is not spending, you should just leave.

Whenever I hear a man saying that he could have any woman he wants because of his money, I feel disrespected. There are enough women who will not date, mate or spend their valuable time with a man just because he is wealthy. There are many women who are either rich themselves or would rather live a modest life instead of dealing with a man they don't like. Don't let men try to convince you that they are the "real deal" because they have a private jet, millions in cash, mansions, etc. If they are extremely unattractive, short-tempered, disrespectful, dishonest, etc., then they are not the real deal. I think there's nothing wrong with receiving money, gifts or favors from a man who doesn't meet your manly criteria. However, being in a relationship with someone for whom you have no positive feelings is a bad decision.

I dated several men like that. It didn't bother me since I didn't have to share a house with them and I wasn't having sex with them. I imagine how difficult it might be for certain women to deal with this situation. I would never be in a real relationship with a man to whom I'm not genuinely attracted, or whose values don't align with mine, or a man with a mindset and a character that are not conducive to the act of being kind to others in spite of his wealth. You should adopt this approach as well.

There's so much wealth in the United States and there are enough young, handsome and wealthy men who will treat you better than an ugly, short-tempered man. So aim for a real *"real deal"* whatever that means to you and do not compromise. A high value man, for me, is someone to whom I am physically attracted; someone who is not only financially successful but also successful in making me feel happier.

## KINGS

A king is a man who is willing to share his wealth with the woman he loves. Kings admire your hustle as a young woman trying to make the American dream happen. A king is usually a man who is physically attractive, on your personal opinion. If you don't have the money to afford the habits and their lifestyle, you should at least invest in living in a nice neighborhood. Living where the rich reside can increase your chances of finding a king. You can find rich men in stores like Lowe's, Home Depot, Whole Foods, or just by walking around at the mall. You can meet rich men through your profession as well. For example, you can find them as a waitress, bartender, or receptionist.

There are many types of rich men that you will find on your journey. Some men got lucky once and are still living off their returns. This might be the case for lottery winners and gamblers. There are men who got divorced and received a good amount of money afterward. The rarest types are the gay and bisexual men that want a mate for public validation. This kind of man is rare because people today are less concerned about the opinions of others.

Some men inherit their wealth from their parents. These men have never proven that they were worthy of their wealth, so they tend to be deeply insecure despite how much money they have. Most of them feel inferior to their parents because they aren't as accomplished or successful on their own. These men tend to be underachievers and have nothing going on for themselves, so all they want to do is spend time with you. They are easy prey, and because they seek validation, you should use words of affirmation to inflate this type of man's ego.

## PAWNS

Pawns are rich men or upper-middle-class men who have money but are not willing to spend on women. There's the "humble type" of rich that do not flash what they have. In most cases they are cheap and when they are cheap, they value feelings over things. They only spend when they feel absolutely amazed by a woman. She needs to be almost physically and morally perfect to get anything from them. Along with being grateful for the least expensive gift, you have to be like a precious diamond that they've found.

There's the "real cheap" man who might ask you to sign a prenuptial agreement. Ginie Sayles, author of *How to Marry the Rich: The Rich Will Marry Someone, Why Not You?*, says in her book that the intentions and the character of the man who requires you to sign such a document is repugnant.

> *"Know the underlying psychology of a prenuptial agreement. Most people talk in noble terms of fairness. Rarely is that the motive for a prenuptial agreement. Control, selfishness, fear, sometimes even cruelty may be hidden in the talk of fairness. In the case of duress, when you are presented with the prenuptial agreement at the time of taking your marriage vows, a rich man is using embarrassment as a weapon against you to force you, to manipulate you to agree to the rich man's terms. It is easy to see that the rich man who puts you into this situation or who insists on an unfair prenuptial agreement is attempting to create a parent- child dependency in the relationship."*

Unfortunately, wealthy and stingy men are the most common type of pawns. There are many of them available because women don't want to deal with them. They require too much and give little in return. You have to be physically and mentally awesome. They commit easily, stick around, and are willing to help you get to the next level. I now regret the time wasted with them because I realized later that I didn't need to deal with a cheap man.

A lot of women will deal with pawns before they can find their king. You might have to work on it for years. In the book *Shanghai Girls: Uncensored & Unsentimental* by Mina Hanbury-Tenison, a Shanghai girl named Lan Lan draws back the curtain to reveal how to use your feminine wiles to attract a desirable and wealthy man. Lan Lan teaches that Chinese and many other Asian girls are known for marrying multiple times. Each time, they marry a richer man. Many of these girls come from an extremely poor background, and they need to marry more than once until they can find a man who will give them the world. The lesson is to start where you are and not to waste any time. Over time, you can get to where you want to be.

Sometimes you need to date a nurse first in order to be invited to the parties where you can meet a doctor. The type of man that you are looking for earns enough money to take care of you and himself fully, plus can meet your wants and needs. He needs to be far enough into his career to make a good income or own his own business. He doesn't need to be older than you, but he needs to be in love with you. In reality your green card sponsor is only required to make a minimum of 21,775 United States dollars yearly. You don't need to find a rich man.

## PEASANTS

Peasants are men who openly live in poverty without any plans to take themselves out of it. Peasants also pretend to be rich to impress women, but they are not in the middle class and can't even help themselves. It is important to know how to identify someone that lives in poverty because if you marry this type of man, you will suffer the consequences. To remove broke men from your options, you need to know how to spot one first.

- If he rents his house instead of owning it, it's a sign he is not rich.

- If he buys used expensive cars, sleeps on a cheap mattress, or lives in an old house, he is broke.

- If the man you are dating doesn't hire other people to fix his car, do plumbing, or fix things in his home, he's not rich.

Wealthy people delegate daily tasks so that they can focus on what makes them money. Take note that in the United States majority of men don't know how to change a lamp bulb, and they have no idea how to fix their own cars, install furniture or even put the pieces of a dinner table together. That's why they delegate tasks, and not because they are wealthy.

Another way to know that a man is broke is when he is a political fanatic. Men who are fans of politics usually like to talk about who has the power, or where the power resides.

Power is not something they can have, so they can only theorize about it. They often harbor an inferiority complex that makes them feel like the world is under the control of something or someone they can't beat. The same goes for men obsessed with sports; they praise winners to feel connected to their stardom, and to make up for the fact that they are not shining.

If a man has a gambling problem, he is broke. Gambling, poker tournaments and lottery ticket purchases, for example, have been an addiction of the poor for a long time. Gambling is a result of a mind that operates in poverty. It is the belief of the possibility of getting rich overnight without any hard work. Poor people believe the rich got lucky and that the world is extremely unfair. It is true that nobody gets rich by working long hours in a regular job and saving every penny. But no one gets rich without being persistent, consistent, and committed to a goal worth achieving. What a man does daily is more important than any big project or idea he has in his mind for a brief moment. Poor men can't manage being committed to a goal for the long term.

Another way to figure out if he is not the right man for you is when he prefers to invite you for dates where there's little to no chance of spending money. He might take you on dates like going to the beach, parks, museums, or getting ice cream. It is common for those peasant men to expect you to follow them in their masculine activities like football games, hiking, boating, and camping. Those kinds of men not only refuse to spend money on women, but they don't like women with the same intensity as a masculine man does. These men don't do much to impress you, so do not fall for this type of man.

## THE JEWELS OF JULIANA

Juliana was a beautiful twenty-four-year-old girl from Colombia who married a fifty-year-old American man named Jeffrey. Juliana followed all of the rules to set herself up for success. She didn't have sex with Jeffrey before marriage. Juliana stood in her feminine power. She requested provisions and protections before marriage, and Jeffrey agreed to all of her terms.

Once they got married, which originally seemed to be the perfect outcome for them both, Jeffrey turned out to be an absolute nightmare for Juliana. He had agreed to provide financially for her, but he knew that his income wasn't high enough and that he could barely afford to take care of himself. Jeffrey provided the cheapest lifestyle for Juliana. He would never give Juliana any money to spend on herself. On her birthday, Christmas, or Valentine's Day, she would only receive a card or a love letter. Then Juliana started to notice that Jeffrey was receiving numerous phone calls and mail from collection agencies.

She soon realized that the little money he made went towards sustaining his addictions. Jeffrey was addicted to all kinds of gambling, including card games and playing the lottery. He started to ask Juliana for money and because she wanted to help him, she loaned him money. He would ask her for more and more. It summed up into a big amount of money that he never repaid her.

Desperate to get out of the relationship, she called a lawyer that advised her to get a divorce. She was afraid that if she divorced Jeffrey, it would affect her application for immigrant benefits. If she filed for a divorce, she would probably have to go back to Colombia. Once Juliana applied for immigrant benefits, the USCIS started meticulously tracking every step she took within the USA. If Juliana had abandoned her process, she would probably have received a letter from the USCIS asking her to leave the country right away. She felt miserable in the relationship, but she chose to stay until the end. She got her green card but ended up in debt because of how much money she had to lend her husband.

Marrying Jeffery was a harsh lesson. Just because a man says he will provide for you doesn't mean he's capable of doing it. Never marry a man who doesn't make enough income. Notwithstanding, the success of a relationship is not entirely based on the economic aspect. There are so many other things to consider before closing the deal with an American citizen in the marriage business.

Love and money are two different things. Therefore do not accept love from a man who cannot provide financially. When a man has low income, some women tend to accept the man's devotion and obsession as fair compensation. In my experience, some men will become extra submissive, always available and super serving when they are not offering you money.

It feels good to have a slave taking care of you. But remember that if he doesn't give you money, it is because he doesn't love you. If he doesn't have money at all, not even for himself, it is because he doesn't love himself.

# CHAPTER 6

# CHECKMATE AND THE CHESS PLAYERS

## DATING INSIDE

Despite being more expensive, dating outside of the Internet is usually worth the effort because online dating has such a bad reputation. When you are on the Internet, you automatically blend in with everyone else, including those who are there to scam and trick others for money.

It is worth searching outside of the Internet but it takes money to spend time with the type of man that would be ideal for you. You might need to travel to upscale places, take first-class flights, or have a country club membership. If you can give it a try, you can meet rich men in membership clubs, on golf courses, at major sporting events, casinos, yacht clubs or marinas, airplane hangars, expensive car dealerships like Ferrari or Lamborghini, or high-end restaurants at lunchtime.

Meeting someone in person also means that you will talk to people face-to-face. A woman or man can be super-attractive, but if they open their mouth and have unattractive teeth, it can be a real turnoff. Equally important is hygiene because bad breath is a significant turnoff.

## GETTING STARTED

If you date as many people as you possibly can at the same time, your chances of getting married faster will increase exponentially. So don't put all your hopes in one basket. The more you date, the greater your chances of marrying someone increase. Never commit to having one boyfriend at a time because you are single until the day you sign your official marriage documents. The more you keep your dating life full, the more desirable you are to a man.

Dating a man in the same geographic area as you is also beneficial because during holidays like Christmas, Thanksgiving, and Easter everybody feels more sensitive and lonely and more depressed being alone, so those are perfect times to start looking for houses with your boyfriend. Men from the USA have residence in many developing countries. They live in Colombia, Brazil, Costa Rica, etc. Those men might be close to where you live right now without needing to travel.

In her book *How to Marry the Rich: The Rich Will Marry Someone, Why Not You?* Ginie Sayles teaches that the holidays are a perfect time to close the deal on marriage because marrying during this time will make him feel more comfortable because the wedding will seem like part of the celebratory spirit. The exchange of rings is part of the spiritual momentum and sentimentality of the season. I suggest prioritizing the marriage in the courthouse before you plan a beautiful ceremony.

If the man you want to marry has friends that might interfere in your relationship, like advising him that he might be marrying too fast, introduce his friends to potential dates you know. If your man fears being judged or doesn't want to disappoint anyone by marrying you, suggest a small ceremony. Tell him you want it to be special for the both of you, and the fact that it is so fast makes the event more exciting. Throw in a sexy wink.

Dating in real life will also give you the task of seducing not only your fiancé but also all his friends and family. Seduction is the use of charm or temptation consciously to get something out of someone.

## DATING OUT

If, for whatever reason, you cannot make the trip to the USA on your own and you want or need a man to come and pick you up in your country, sign up for online dating. All you have to do is upload your pictures, make your biography, and negotiate the arrangement to get married to your potential spouse. In this case, you can do a background check on the man you are dating and trust your instinct about the person.

The second option is to hire a dating company to connect you with candidates. This is the safest option because the companies are assisted by the International Marriage Broker Regulation Act (IMBRA) to protect American citizens and immigrants from the risks of meeting over the Internet.

These companies scan the users and take care of the visa process for you. A good matchmaking company can save you time and headache by researching a potential spouse. They do a background check and also find out information about the suitor's previous marriages, if they have any children, and all previous residences. The international matchmaking organization only discloses information about the couple after they apply for the visa K-1. IMBRA makes your relationship feel more serious, and it has been proven to result in marriages that are not dysfunctional. Another bonus of using a matchmaking company is that the men who prefer to hire those companies to find a mate tend to be wealthier.

## GETTING STARTED

Your picture is the most critical part of your dating profile. Looks are everything when it comes to online dating. It is important to catch a man's eye and make a good first impression. I had my pictures professionally taken, and it was the best thing I did because it attracted more quality men.

If a man asks you for a nude picture, don't ever send it to him. If he requests for phone sex or video call sex, don't do it. That's what sex phone operators and *Only Fans* influencers are paid for.

For online dating, the first thing to do is to write a great profile name. Patti Stanger, author of *Become Your Own Matchmaker: 8 Easy Steps for Attracting Your Perfect Mate*, advises you to pick a provocative and flattering name like *Sultry Brunette*, *Bi-coastal Beauty*, or *Sugar and Spice*. It's your time to shine, so be provocative. Put *licious* at the end of your name, like *Lindalicious*, or incorporate your best feature, as in *Velvet Voiced Vixen* or *Blue Eyed Bella*. Write a happy, fun profile by using exciting words such as "playful," "energetic," "fun," "upbeat," "positive," "fit," "creative," "attractive," and "sharp." Millionaire escort and author Lydia Dupra shares her secrets to success in the taboo business of being a high-class escort. In her book, *Sugar or Hooker: The Complete Guide to Escorting (Vol. 1)*, she recommends creating a great online headline like the one written below:

> *I have a bubbly/witty personality and I love to give as much as I receive... I can't wait for our first encounter. Yes that's 100% me in these recently taken pics. If I don't look like my pictures, I'll buy you a drink.*

Dupra also recommends that you check out a man's information online and do a background check using verify-him.com. To prove he is legit, ask him for reference numbers and contacts of his friends and family and chat with them. When you meet him in person, take a picture of his driver's license and his credit or debit card to see if it matches with his ID. If he is okay with you having his ID in your phone or your computer, it is easier to trust him.

When you write the *About You* section, don't be too brief. Also, the word "generous" must be avoided at all cost. Just assume men already know they must be generous. You don't want to say that you are looking for a man who will give you financial benefits, but you can use different wording that is respectful and means the same thing. You can use phrases like, *looking for a man at the top of his game* and *someone who loves his work and is successful.* When you write about your interests, list upscale hobbies like fine wine, gourmet dining, golf, tennis, and boating. Patti Stanger, author of *Become Your Own Matchmaker: 8 Easy Steps for Attracting Your Perfect Mate*, recommends that instead of saying you are looking for a husband, you can say, *I'm looking for a wonderful man to spend my life with* or *I am looking for a special guy to share my life with.*

It is easy to lose contact with someone you have been chatting online. To make it work, you have to be organized and disciplined. It is common to see people in long-distance relationships staying on the phone all night because the couple is trying to compensate for not seeing each other in person. In the beginning, start talking to him on the phone for a maximum of fifteen minutes. Give the man an excuse that makes you appear interesting because you have to get off the phone. For example, you can tell him you are headed to the gym, going to get a massage, going to get your nails done, or meeting a friend. Never say you have to take care of household chores or watch TV.

Another thing you can do in the beginning is to send him funny pictures or selfies. Pick a time at night or a few hours after he is off work and without making any agreement with him, just call at the same time. As the relationship matures, you can stay on the phone or video call with him for forty minutes to an hour. If he calls you outside of the time you are committed to, pick up the phone, be sweet, but don't talk for more than a few minutes.

# CHAPTER 7
# THE MASTER STRATEGY

The most difficult part is before marriage. After marriage you pretty much don't need to do anything because men will almost never divorce their wives no matter what. Seduction is the use of charm or temptation to get something from someone. Robert Greene, author of *The Art of Seduction*, points out that by idealizing your targets, you will make them idealize you back. Idealize their president, their food, and the American way. Celebrate every American holiday without holding back. Wear costumes, host get-togethers, and learn all the related songs.

To be efficient in seduction, never express doubts about the relationship you expect to result in marriage. Show an attitude that you already know the man loves you and would do anything for you. Use his name and credit cards, put yourself on his insurance, receive mail at his address, and act like he is already yours. You must feel secure in his love, even if you think he is not even close to loving you. As soon as he says he is in love with you, never express doubt. Say you love him too in a very gentle way. If people don't tell each other that they are in love, the relationship will never last. You must get him to say "I love you" often, and you must declare it often as well. Cherish your relationship and never criticize it.

## LOVE AND RACE

When it comes to women, there are physical attributes that are sexually attractive to American men. In general, they prefer white, skinny, long-haired women, according to author Lydia Dupra. She shares that the order of attractiveness of women in the USA is first white women, second Latinas, then black women, and finally Asian women. The beauty and fashion industry promote the image of fair-skinned women as ideal, and popular marriage agencies advertise their businesses with those beauty standards in mind. These companies post pictures of blonde, fair-skinned women on their websites to attract more subscribers.

## CULTURAL DIFFERENCES

Starting a relationship and falling in love with a person from a different culture is a growing experience. This will be an amazing adventure, and you have a lot to look forward to. In this chapter, I will detail how you can use stereotypes to your advantage during the stages of attracting an American partner. Right now, I want to show you how to overcome cultural differences in a relationship.

Be open to learning and growing with your partner. Focus on what you have in common. It can be a great experience to teach each other about your cultures by sharing new foods, traditions, sports, holidays, and ways of thinking. Secondly, as a couple, you will grow inter-culturally. It will make you question the beliefs imposed upon you in your own childhood. It will make you see how easy it is to change a belief or state of mind that does not serve you. Thirdly, being a foreigner makes you appear innocent to his friends and family who really like you. Things you might say or do, like being inappropriate, obnoxious or loud, for example, will not be taken seriously. I noticed that it is easier to be accepted by your lover when you are expected to think completely different from the start. Ultimately, love is also acceptance.

## EUROPEAN COQUETTES

In the book *The Art of Seduction*, Robert Greene teaches that different types of personalities lead to different styles in seduction. He calls *Coquettes* women who possess an ability to delay gratification by implementing a back-and-forth movement between hope and frustration. Greene says, *"The greatest power in seduction is your ability to turn away, to make others come after you, delaying their satisfaction."*

Coquettes hold the cards because they are considered out of reach. In the same way, the perception with Russian women is that they are elegant, sophisticated, and mysterious. They are so alluring that men prefer to treat them with respect for their pure and virtuous character. Men don't rush them into intimacy too soon because they are afraid those women will stop letting men court their favor.

## RUSSIAN BRIDES

The marriage market in Russia has been the most successful because it presents Russian women as being the dream of every man and, so far, has been winning over all the other nationalities at the dating game.

Men from North America, Australia, and Western Europe perceive a Russian woman as being a female born in countries that were part of the old Soviet Union: Russia, Ukraine, Belarus, Kazakhstan, Georgia, Armenia, etc. Walter Parchomenko, author of *Ukrainian & Russian Bride Guide: Dangers and Joys Awaiting Western Men*, says that these women are famous for their allure. Many are long-legged blondes with soulful eyes and high cheekbones. Their physical appearance has a strongly seductive effect on men. To excite and attract American men to her business, a top Ukrainian blogger called Krystyna described Ukrainian women on her international dating website as the following:

> *"Ukrainian women are the most beautiful in the world. The obvious reason women from Ukraine can attract a man from America is due to their exotic beauty. Women from Ukraine have a tra-*

*ditional American beauty, along with sensual beauty hard to find in American girls, and they have this sensuality without being sleazy. Women from Ukraine also appeal to Western men because they are taught to be completely respectful to the men in their life. Women from Ukraine can be as strong willed as American women, but they generally display their strong will in a more controlled manner than American women do. Women from Ukraine enjoy being housewives, and they excel at housewife duties. The beauty of Ukrainian women, combined with their love of supporting the men in their life, makes them the perfect companion for Western men, and that is why Western men cannot resist them. They possess values so rare to find in Western society. Their attentive loving ways will charm you and their feminine well-kept appearance will captivate you. These Russian women are marriage-minded, highly educated, loyal, intelligent, beautiful, and loving. There are no equals to Russian brides for faithfulness and loyalty."*

Ukraine once had highly fertile soil, so the country received the reputation for being the breadbasket of Europe, as Parchomenko points out. Today, the same place is considered the bride basket for foreign men. During the wars between Russia and Ukraine (2014–2017), both countries lost a big part of their male population in combat. Suddenly, the marriage agencies saw a business opportunity in the dating market. To attract more foreign men, the companies began to advertise on their websites the immense disparity in numbers between men and women in those countries. They reported 10 million fewer men than women in Russia and 1.5 million more women than men in Ukraine. Soon after, there was an influx of foreign men traveling from all over the world, especially Americans, to find Ukrainian and Russian romantic partners.

## RUSSIAN STRATEGY

Many agencies introduce foreign men to Russian and Ukrainian women. Those agencies do background checks on the candidates to make sure they meet the expectations of the girls. They check for previous marriages, trafficking, drug charges, arrests, and other illegal activities. Parchomenko shares that it is a misconception that the men who seek out these women are old losers who are not good enough for the women in their own country. He says many of them have good-paying jobs and can be business owners and doctors. He says, *"The only real losers are the men who never find the courage to pursue their dream."*

The process starts with foreign men signing up with the marriage agencies to meet Russian women. One of the most popular agencies costs ninety-nine dollars a month for a subscription. Russian women rarely speak English, so the chatting services charge a fee to translate every message and twenty-five dollars for each email letter. After a few months, men have spent thousands to communicate with them online. The men can also send gifts, fruits baskets, flowers, chocolate for an additional fee.

After the online courting, which can take months and sometimes years, foreign men travel to meet the women in person for the first time. The marriage agencies throw parties and events in Odessa, Ukraine, and cities in Russia. The meeting can take place at the event hosted by the agency or the couple can meet at an upscale restaurant after a party has ended. Typically, there is an interpreter that charges a fee of about thirty dollars an hour. After foreign men talk to them, they are expected to pay for the woman's transportation to get back home.

According to Parchomenko, it is not unusual to see a foreign man propose marriage right after a week of meeting his Russian angel for the first time. However, sometimes men get disappointed by the woman they came to meet. The man's disappointment can come from not getting to have sex with the woman after putting in so much time and money. The men claim that the Russian women make promises to be intimate with them, but they never deliver. Men rescue them financially only to have a new emergency come up, like a sick parent, the loss of a job, or even the need for grocery money. They state that the women only need one more bill paid and soon just another and another. It becomes a never-ending requirement. When men stop giving them money, the Russian women cut the communication, and sex never comes.

If you are an eastern European woman looking to come to the USA and marry an American man, your chances of finding many good suitable candidates are very high. You can take your time to choose the best fit and get him to invest time and money into the online relationship because as he invests in you, his level of interest only increases, and you will have a higher chance of securing a relationship that will last for a long time or as long as you want it to last. If he believes you are not talking to anyone else besides him, he will commit to you.

Many men are skeptical when meeting women online, especially if you are way out of their league. As a beautiful, high-value woman, you need to make him feel secure in your feelings for him and make him believe you are completely serious. He needs to be confident that you are willing to come to the USA and marry him. If you already live in the USA, the same rules apply, so you must be clear that you will not change your mind.

## THE STAR

In his book *The Art of Seduction*, Robert Greene describes another type of seductress as the *Star*. Stars, just like the Latinas, have a glittering and elusive presence. They are known for smiling, dancing, and being musical, which causes men to want to watch them. Stars love to transform themselves into glittering objects and stand out from the crowd. They have voluminous hair and unique, big, handmade, noisy jewelry. Greene describes a Star as a woman that reflects and exudes the eccentricity of your most imaginative fantasies and dreams. Stars intrigue men because it seems that there's always more to see.

The numerous Latina immigrants in the USA today are the result of massive immigration. Latinas are women from Central and South America. The influx of Latinas to the USA has been increasing each year.

## LATINA STEREOTYPES
The style and personality of Latinas are marked by an ambiguity between feminine and masculine behaviors.

The feminine actions of Latinas portray them as domestic, submissive caregivers with natural maternal instincts. A Latina's masculine behaviors create the perception of a strong libido that sometimes surpasses men's capacity to satisfy them. The feminine perception attracts men who want to benefit from their cooking, cleaning, and caregiving style. The masculine characteristics attract men who want to have sex with them to experience their unique sensuality.

## LATINA STRATEGY

For Latina women to attract an American man's interest, she needs to make herself look more like a white American woman. The most successful in seduction are the Latinas who have slim bodies, take special care of their hair by relaxing it to keep it straight, dye their hair as light as they can, and keep their skin as light as possible by avoiding tanning. Marriage companies are not typically as helpful as they are in Russia. That's why you should promote yourself on social media.

## ASIAN STRATEGY

Asian women love to dress and look so hyper-feminine that they even resemble a female child. They like to bleach their skin and keep their body thin. They are known for their refined grace, beautiful skin, small size, demure manner, long hair, and feminine ways. An Asian woman is often objectified and can be expected to be smaller and thinner than any other ethnic group. There is a stereotype of Asian men being softer and reserved, and it is assumed that Asian women have natural hyper-femininity.

If you are an Asian woman, use this stereotype as part of your strategy to get the attention of men of other races. Act like you crave masculinity. An American man will feel like a knight in shining armor by marrying you because he rescues you with his masculinity.

As an Asian woman, it is to your advantage to find men attracted to younger women. However, there are bad stereotypes as well. First, men think Asian women are culturally conditioned to care for their parents when they get older, so they expect that their Asian wives will have no issues taking care of them.

Filipina women are known for having a darker skin complexion and are also sought out by American men in the marriage market. Their youthful beauty and the fact that English is the Philippines' second official language helps them connect with American suitors. As a Filipina woman, use your femininity to attract an American man, and keep your standards high. Filipina women are seen as highly sexualized but make sure you don't provide sex until after marriage.

## AFRICAN DANDIES

In *The Art of Seduction*, Robert Greene introduces the *Dandy* as a seductress who casts a spell by using the opposite gender's same behaviors. The fascination to a man is her independence and capability of detachment. Men are attracted to Dandies because of their ambiguous and obscure personas. Seductresses break the prejudice of sexual behavioral roles. Like Dandies, African women are seen as being masculine and feminine at the same time. They are perceived as masculine when they are opinionated and strong heroes, but they are feminine when they are perceived as being the mother source of all other races of women. They are mysterious, naturally beautiful and fun, and men are drawn to them.

## AFRICAN WOMEN

The world can learn a great deal from African women because they have endured a vast amount of abuse, racism, and sexism from individuals and institutions. Despite these challenges, they have risen and become successful in the corporate world. Nowadays, African women have become highly educated. Many African women dominate government sectors, occupations considered to be pink-collar employment.

Unlike African-American women, there is an expectation that African women will be more traditional and keep the old standard of femininity and masculinity. African women are expected to cook, clean, and to be obedient to their husbands. However, African-American women are often seen as career-oriented and not traditional.

## AFRICAN WOMEN STRATEGY

In the book *Black Women in Interracial Relationships: In Search of Love and Solace*, Kellina Craig-Henderson points out three major stereotypes of black women. The first is called the 'Mommy.' This personality is docile, happy, and eager to please. She is large, overweight, dark-skinned and big-breasted, has wide hips, unattractive, and is also asexual. The second personality is called the 'Jezebel.' They are hypersexual and promiscuous in a way that lacks class. The third stereotype is the 'Sapphire.' The perception is that she is critical, hostile, confrontational, difficult, sassy, bossy, uncooperative, and emasculative. This stereotype perceives white men as being in love with those bossy characteristics, while black men would find those same traits unattractive. This dynamic justifies interracial relationships between white men and black women.

A black woman is seen as more evolved because of the stereotype that they're strong, bossy, and obstinate. That's why the strategy for women coming from Africa to live in the USA is to play the complete opposite role. Be submissive and less outspoken when dealing with either black or white men. Once you win the heart of the man you seek, you can begin to assert more dominance and then show your intelligence.

Black women are among the largest groups of females into sadomasochism and sexual and financial domination who profit from men. To this type of woman, men are considered cash slaves, pig pay, and human ATMs. A black dominatrix known as Mistress Velvet incorporates the study of black feminist literature when working with her white submissive customers while she is whipping their naked bodies.

There's a lot of guilt on American men's shoulders due to slavery from the past. Some white-privileged men feel like they need to make amends to African women for how they were treated. When a man worships a black female involved in domination, it's a way to give them reparations. It's also a way for men to feel good about themselves, whether the woman is engaged in domination or not. When men think they are doing good deeds, they feel better about themselves. When a man can see a better version of himself, he feels successful. Dating a black woman can bring him a sense of success.

As a black woman, it's a good idea to date every race, including the white men as well. Lisa Marble, author of *How to Be Irresistible to White Men: Interracial Dating Secrets of Asian Women, Black Women Who Swirl Should Know*, teaches in her book that on a dating website, to get the attention of white men, you need to put out clues. You can say that you have a thing for blue, grey, or green eyes in your profile. You can mention you like a man with blonde, red, or light-colored hair. You could also mention liking an Italian accent or a modern-day cowboy. This method is a subtle way of letting men know you are looking for someone who is Caucasian. If there is a particular celebrity you find attractive, you can reference that you like men who have that celebrity's looks or vibe. For example, you can say you like the "George Clooney clones."

Author Lisa Marble also recommends that all women of color who are looking for a foreign white man should state very clearly that they love to learn about different cultures and that they love to travel. She also recommends that you write something in the language of the man you wish to marry.

## WINNING THE GAME

Chess can only be won by a checkmate. Winning happens when one player threatens the other player's King. At this point in the game, the king can't move to any other squares, and no other pieces can protect him without being captured. To win the Green Card Chess Game is to win in love and marriage. After reading this book, you should now have the tools and strategy to win your opponent's heart and get your Green Card. It's been said that the king is the most important chess piece on the board, but the queen is the most powerful. You are a queen. You are powerful. I challenge you to win the Green Card Chess Game!

# CHAPTER 8

# CONCLUSION

Thank you for reading this book! In no particular order, here's how to get your green card and win at love and marriage.

1. Don't come across as a green card hunter.

2. Don't marry just for the green card.

3. Don't marry just for money.

4. Don't marry or have a romantic relationship with a man whom you are not physically attracted to.

5. Only have sex after marriage.

6. Be feminine.

7. Have high standards.

8. Be patient.

9. Be appreciative.

10. Improve your social skills.

11. Take care of your mental and physical wellbeing.

12. Be loving and kind.

13. Be genuinely attracted to the personality type of the person you are marrying.

14. Don't sabotage your dreams and don't let anyone do it neither.

15. Don't marry someone that is financially challenged.

16. Use the opportunity of being financially provided for to bring about your talents to the world, not your workforce.

# ABOUT THE AUTHOR

Michely's mother moved to Spain at the end of the '90s where she lived for over 15 years. Her mother was able to buy a home and a business for her family so that she could provide for her three children. In 2010, Michely's mother married her current foreign husband. Her mother moved back to Brazil, her original country, in 2013.

In 2010, Michely's father began dating a woman in the United States through the internet and he eventually married her. In 2011, her father moved to the United States to build a family with his American fiancée and her daughter.

Michely had always dreamed about living in the United States and at the end of 2014, she moved to Florida to live with her father, step-mother, and step-sister.

Michely holds the title of Miss Texas-Brazil USA 2018 and 2019 and uses this platform to inspire women and men to believe in themselves and their value. She motivates women and men to fight for their dreams and beliefs. She wants men and women to feel beautiful and to see beauty in others.

# REFERENCES

Abrams, Kerry. *"Immigration Law and the Regulation of Marriage."* Minnesota Law Review 9 (2007): 1624.

Hanrahan, James Allen. *A Life of Love: How to Create Relationships You Want*. Place of Publication Not Identified: Publisher Not Identified, 2012, p. 75–76.

*"Don't Give It Up."* Performed by SheRaSeven. YouTube.com. June 15, 2018. https://www.youtube.com/watch?v=XIzPZjxz8DM

Allen, Patricia. *Getting to "I Do": The Secret to Doing Relationships Right!* New York: Avon Books, 1995, p. 214.

Brown, Sandra L. *How to Spot a Dangerous Man Before You Get Involved: Describes 8 Types of Dangerous Men, Gives Defense Strategies and a Red Alert Checklist for Each*. New York: Hunter House, 2011.

Sayles, Ginie. *How to Marry the Rich: The Rich Will Marry Someone, Why Not You?* GeMar Publications, 2009, pp. 425–16.

Lan, Lan, and Mina Hanbury-Tenison. *Shanghai Girls: Uncensored & Unsentimental: How to Marry Up and Stay There.* Hong Kong: Make-Do, 2010, p. 30.

Stanger, Patti, and Lisa Johnson Mandell. *Become Your Own Matchmaker: 8 Easy Steps for Attracting Your Perfect Mate.* London: Simon & Schuster, 2012, p. 53.

Dupra, Lydia. *Sugar or Hooker: The Complete Guide to Escorting. Vol. 1.* BookBaby, 2017, p. 58.

Greene, Robert, and Joost Elffers. *The Art of Seduction.* New York: Penguin Books, 2014, p. 219.

Parchomenko, Walter. *Ukrainian & Russian Bride Guide: Dangers & Joys Awaiting Western Men.* AWeakAm Books, 2013, p. 25.

Russian & Ukrainian Dating Sites Reviews. February 21, 2021. Accessed March 4, 2021. https://www.ukrainiandatingstories.com/.

"Ethnic and Racial Minorities & Socioeconomic Status." American Psychological Association. Accessed March 13, 2021. https://www.apa.org/pi/ses/resources/publications/minorities.

"Number of Black families with a single mother in the United States from 1990 to 2019." Statista. January 20, 2021. Accessed March 14, 2021. https://www.statista.com/statistics/205106/number-of-black-families-with-a-female-householder-in-the-us/.

"Rate of imprisonment in the United States in 2018, by race and gender." Statista. October 7, 2020. Accessed March 14, 2021. https://www.statista.com/statistics/818001/rate-of-imprisonment-in-the-us-by-race-and-gender/.

"Modern Dating as a Black Woman." Omnia. August 15, 2019. Accessed March 14, 2021. https://omnia.sas.upenn.edu/story/modern-dating-black-woman.

Craig-Henderson, Kellina M. *Black Women in Interracial Relationships: In Search of Love and Solace.* Oxford: Routledge, 2017, p. 108.

Marble, Lisa. *How to Be Irresistible to White Men: Interracial Dating Secrets of Asian Women Black Women Who Swirl Should Know.* Place of Publication Not Identified: LM Publishing, 2013, p. 50.

*Men Are From Mars, Women Are From Venus.* John Gray. 1992. HarperCollins.

Milton Keynes UK
Ingram Content Group UK Ltd.
UKHW021838240823
427419UK00016B/506

9 798822 921351